My Wish for You

One Wish for You

Celebrating the Women in Our Lives

Celia Whitler

ABINGDON PRESS
Nashville

ONE WISH FOR YOU

ISBN 978-1-426-70020-0

09 10 11 12 13 14 15 16 17 18 – 10 9 8 7 6 5 4 3 2 1
PRINTED IN MEXICO

This book is dedicated to my friend Kathleen Baskin-Ball.
You are an inspiration. Many of these songs were inspired by your life,
your hope, and your witness.

And to my husband, Ron, and my wonder boys, Max and Zach. I love
you, and I like you, and I am so blessed to walk my days with you.

Thanks to:
Lesa Allen – You read each word, laughed, cried, and questioned it at just
the right times. Thanks for being a friend who checks my homework.

Meg Maddox – You are my reminder that "happily ever after" is real.

Photography shoot: Russ Rohrer, photographer; Kelly Green, hair and
makeup; Dianna Maher, great house

The incredible production team: Susan, Billie, Anna, Marcia

All the women in my life who have made me better today than I was
yesterday, talked me down from a ledge, loved me through it all, and
modeled a life worth loving and living.

The lyrics to "One Wish for You" are inside the pages of this book, along with selected
Scriptures and a few of my thoughts about journey and friendship.

Enjoy the journey – Celia

You are a mother, daughter, sister, aunt, grandmother, neighbor, accountant, Sunday school teacher, coach, sister-in-law, lawyer, rock star, songwriter, housewife, room mother, principal, cafeteria lady, teacher, artist, mentor, choir director, youth pastor, best friend, author, boss, senator, chaplain, singer, receptionist, mother-in-law, **and so much more.**

You've inspired me, changed me, laughed with me, prayed for me, held me, bandaged me, risked with me, listened to me, written notes to me, helped me move, howled at the moon with me, walked down the aisle with me, blessed me, picked up shells with me, cried with me, shared your heart with me, and encouraged me every day in every way. You can't seem to figure what all the fuss is about, because you were just being you. I love you. I want to be more like you. I see glimpses of all that is good in life in you, and I celebrate that our paths crossed. I'm better because of you. Thank you for teaching me how to believe, wish, dream, sing, risk, dare, and fly. Thank you for being there. Thank you for always being my home.

Thank you, for being you.

If I had one wish

May he grant you your heart's desire,
and fulfill all your plans.

— Psalm 20:4

Tiny wishes hold enormous possibilities!

I'd wish for you

So I tell you, whatever you ask for in prayer, believe that you have received it, and it will be yours.

— Mark 11:24

faith

hope

Hope for all that is now and all that is to come.

You'd know only love
will see you through

And now faith, hope, and love abide, these three;
and the greatest of these is love.

— 1 Corinthians 13:13

Love

You teach by example
that love will
see you through.

from morning to morning

Satisfy us in the morning with your
steadfast love,
so that we may rejoice and be glad
all our days.

— Psalm 90:14

You rise each morning
        expecting something new.

You go to bed thankful for the blessings of the day

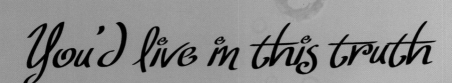

You'd live in this truth

. . . and you will know the truth, and the truth will make you free.

— John 8:32

You know some other truths. Truths like:

Sometimes things are healed, not fixed.

Chocolate is its own food group.

Mascara and caffeine sometimes are all you need to get through the day.

Not living is scarier than dying.

You know time spent with a friend is the most filling part of a meal.

Cake for breakfast and pancakes for dinner make perfect sense to you.

It's never too late to have a happy childhood.

Life isn't fair but you can be.

Being kind takes less energy than not being kind.

If I had one wish

You open your hand,
    satisfying the desire of every living thing.
                                — Psalm 145:16

I wish you'd know
how loved you are.

I'd wish this for you

Some pretend to be rich, yet have nothing;
others pretend to be poor, yet have great wealth.
— Proverbs 13:7

If I could wrap up one present for you for a lifetime . . .
inside would be a wealth of life . . .
in friends, purpose, family, compassion, joy, and love . . .

lots of love.

If I had one dream

For surely I know the plans I have for you, says the Lord, plans for your welfare and not for harm, to give you a future with hope.

— Jeremiah 29:11

I'd dream you grace that brings peace . . . peace in chaos, peace when it's noisy, peace in conflict, peace when life is sorrowful, peace shared with others, peace in solitude, peace that passes all understanding . . . and you know it begins on your street, in your home, inside of you.

I'd dream each day

For everything there is a season, and
a time for every matter under heaven . . .
a time to weep, and a time to laugh;
a time to mourn, and a time to dance . . .
— Ecclesiastes 3:1, 4

I'd dream you a life of simple grace

He has told you, O mortal, what is good;
and what does the LORD require of you
but to do justice, and to love kindness,
and to walk humbly with your God?
— Micah 6:8

You dream of the best and aim for it.

Grace that brings peace to each of your days

Therefore do not worry about tomorrow, for tomorrow
will worry about itself.

— Matthew 6:34, NIV

You let go of things that do not matter.

If had I one dream

. . . the LORD looks on the heart.
— 1 Samuel 16:7

I wish you could see
yourself as I see you.

I'd dream you grace

My grace is sufficient for you . . .

— 2 Corinthians 12:9

You are a light

others see.

If I had one song

O sing to the LORD a new song;
sing to the LORD, all the earth.

— Psalm 96:1

Joy

You lose yourself dancing.

I'd sing of you

I thank my God every time I remember you . . .
— Philippians 1:3

You smile with your eyes.

I'd sing of the big ways your love is true

. . . and live a life of love, just as Christ loved us and gave himself up for us as a fragrant offering and sacrifice to God.

— Ephesians 5:2, NIV

You . . . think with your heart, feel with your mind, speak loudest without words, and touch others with the way you live and love.

I'd sing of the small ways
you do your part

Truly I tell you, just as you did it to one of the least of
these who are members of my family, you did it to me

You really get that the "little" things are the big things.
Things like:

sitting with a friend and having a cup of tea

making your home a place others want to come home to

making forts with blankets

holding hands

bringing a casserole

watching for shooting stars

listening without judging

eating extra sprinkles

sending a card

brushing someone's hair gently

forgiving now rather than later

If I had one song

Make a joyful noise to the LORD,
all the earth;
break forth into joyous song
and sing praises.
— Psalm 98:4

Your life sings.

I'd sing from my heart

How very good and pleasant it is
when kindred live together in unity!
— Psalm 133:1

You are beautiful just as you are today.

One wish

I do not cease to give thanks for you as
I remember you in my prayers.
— Ephesians 1:16

You make a difference.

You believe one voice, one prayer, one person can
make a difference in the world.

One dream

Blessed are the peacemakers, for they
will be called children of God.
— Matthew 5:9

You dream of a world without pain,
hunger, or injustice.
You live to make that happen.

"Can't" is not in your vocabulary.

One song to sing

The LORD your God is with you,
　　he is mighty to save.
He will take great delight in you,
　　he will quiet you with his love,
he will rejoice over you with singing.
　　　　　　　— Zephaniah 3:17, NIV

You live your life one moment at a time.

May your life be
as full as all you bring

I pray that . . . Christ may dwell in your hearts through faith,
as you are being rooted and grounded in love.

— Ephesians 3:16-17

A wish, a dream, a song

I wish you

today you'd have all you gave

. . . and more!

The LORD bless you and keep you;
the LORD make his face to shine upon you,
and be gracious to you;
the LORD lift up his countenance upon you,
and give you peace.

— Numbers 6:24-26

One Wish for You

If I had one wish

I'd wish for you,

You'd know only love

Will see you through

From morning to morning

You'd live in this truth

If I had one wish

I'd wish this for you

One dream

If I had one dream

I'd dream each day

I'd dream you a life

Of simple grace

Grace that brings peace

To each of your days

If I had one dream,

I'd dream you grace

Chorus

One wish

One dream

One song to sing

May your life be as full

As all you bring

I wish you today

You'd have all you gave

One song

If I had one song
I'd sing of you
I'd sing of the big ways
Your love is true
I'd sing of the small ways
You do your part
If I had one song
I'd sing from my heart

Chorus

Most of All You Were There

Busy days, a baby cries
Goodnight moon, whispered lullabies
Sleepless nights, starry skies
A mother loves through weary eyes.

Ponytails, messy meals,
Playground falls, training wheels
First day of school, quick goodbyes
A mother loves through teary eyes.

CHORUS
You loved me first, right from the start
You made the difference, you shape my heart
You gave your life, because you care,
But most of all, you were there.

Time with friends, driving cars
Fragile love, broken hearts
Senior year, up 'til sunrise
A mother loves through patient eyes.

Handsome groom, lovely bride
Life on our own, youthful pride
Visits home, newfound life
A mother loves through happy eyes.

CHORUS

BRIDGE
You gave your life because you care
You showed me how to be there.

CHORUS
You loved me first, right from the start
You made the difference, you shape my heart
You gave your life, because you care,
You taught me how to be there.

'Cause most of all, you were there

Busy days, my baby cries
Now I love through weary eyes.

Come Home

CHORUS

Come home when you're tired and feeling weary,
Come home, find peace and joy and rest.
Come home, feel loving arms around you,
Surrender all your fears, love will meet you here.
Know you're not alone, come home.

CHORUS

Come home when you're tired and feeling weary,
Come home, find peace and joy and rest.
Come home, feel loving arms around you,
Surrender all your fears, love will meet you here.
Know you're not alone, come home.

Softly and tenderly, Jesus is calling,
Calling for you and for me.
See at your doorway, he's waiting and watching,
Watching for you and for me.

CHORUS
Come home when you're tired and feeling weary,
Come home, find peace and joy and rest.
Come home, feel loving arms around you,
Surrender all your fears, love will meet you here.
Know you're not alone, come home.
Surrender all your fears, love will meet you here.
Know you're not alone, come home.

One Wish for You

Celebrating the Women in Our Lives

1. One Wish for You
2. Hope Alive in Me
3. We Believe
4. Most of All You Were There
5. Come Home

Produced by Celia & Ron Whitler, with Ilya Toshinsky
Mixed by Brent Maher
© 2008 Celia & Ron Whitler
Dog Not Included/ASCAP

www.celiamusic.net

Recording team, in order of appearance:

Celia Whitler, Vocals

Ilya Toshinsky, All guitars and other stringed instruments

Ben Phillips, Drums

Craig Young, Bass

Jonell Mosser, Etta Britt, and Billy Tennyson, Background vocals

Ben Phillips, David Axelrod, Charles Yingling, and Kevin Daily, Recording Engineers

Brent Maher, Mixing

Ken Love, Mastering